TRANSFORMATION

Books by Robert A. Johnson

He: Understanding Masculine Psychology

She: Understanding Feminine Psychology

*We: Understanding the Psychology
of Romantic Love*

*Inner Work: Using Dreams and Active
Imagination for Personal Growth*

Ecstasy: Understanding the Psychology of Joy

Femininity Lost and Regained

TRANSFORMATION

Understanding the Three Levels
of Masculine Consciousness

ROBERT A. JOHNSON

HarperSanFrancisco
A Division of HarperCollins*Publishers*

FIRST EDITION

Library of Congress Catalog Card Number 89–45560
ISBN 0–06–250425–8

---

91 92 93 94 95 HAD 10 9 8 7 6 5 4 3 2 1

This edition is printed on acid-free paper that meets the American National Standards Institute Z39.48 Standard.

Contents

Author's Note

Transformation is a study of the evolution of consciousness through its three main levels of development and is predominantly masculine in character. This is not to say that it is the exclusive property of males, and it should be clear that it is as applicable to women as to men. Though each of our three stories depicts the passage of a man through the stages of consciousness, it is woman's journey as much as man's. Since English usage has not yet found a term for those characteristics that apply to both men and women, masculine pronouns and references have been retained throughout.

TRANSFORMATION

Introduction

T radition indicates that three levels of consciousness are available to us: *simple* consciousness, not often seen in our modern technological world; *complex* consciousness, the usual state of educated Western man; and an *enlightened* state of consciousness, known only to a very few individuals, which is the culmination of human evolution and can be attained only by highly motivated people after much work and training.

Proverbs in many languages point out these three levels of consciousness. One story, for instance, relates that the simple man comes home in the evening wondering what's for dinner, the complex man comes home pondering the imponderables of fate, and the enlightened man comes home wondering what's for dinner. Simple man and enlightened man have much in common, including a direct, uncomplicated view of life, and so they react in similar ways. The only true difference between them is that the enlightened man is conscious of his condition, while the simple man is not. Complex man, on the other hand, spends much of his time worrying and often is in a state of anxiety.

A Zen proverb states: "When I was young and free, the mountains were the mountains, the river was the river, the sky was the sky. Then I lost my way, and the mountains were no longer the mountains, the river was no longer the river, the sky was no longer the sky. Then I attained satori (the Zen term for enlightenment), and the mountains were again the mountains, the river was again the river, and the sky was again the sky."

Our biblical tradition takes us from the simple perfection of the Garden of Eden through every imaginable chaos and leads us finally to the heavenly Jerusalem. Again, three levels of consciousness.

Our psychological traditions also validate the existence of these three levels. Fritz Kunkel, a psychotherapist who worked in Los Angeles from the 1930s through the 1950s, observed that human beings proceed from red-blooded to pale-blooded to gold-blooded consciousness, or from simple to superior. This was his simple way of describing the three levels of consciousness open to us. Dr. Esther Harding has pointed out that psychic energy can manifest itself in three ways: as instinct, as ego consciousness, and as investment in the Self. Man evolves from acting instinctively to putting his psychic energy under the control of his ego. Then he must evolve further, to place his psychic energy under the control of the Self, that higher consciousness that is variously called God, enlightenment, satori, or samadhi.

One looks in vain for examples of the man of simple consciousness in our complex Western world. We often project this quality onto dark-skinned minorities and women—and then resent them for it. Writing of his experiences at Walden Pond, Thoreau chronicles a complex man's attempts to regain the simplicity of his life. Our own counterculture movement of the 1960s was an attempt to restore a simplicity and contact with Mother Earth and natural living. Mahatma Gandhi urged India to retain its simple consciousness, symbolized by the spinning wheel. He would have had every Indian live a simple life, spinning his own cloth, cleaning his own house and latrine, and so on. India nicely sidestepped this advice by isolating Gandhi in its pantheon of saints, and his life has little effect on present-day India.

When I first went to India I had been warned of the horrors I would encounter—lepers, corpses on the street, poverty, maimed children, and beggars. All of this was true, and I withstood the impact of the darkness as best I could. I had not been warned, however, of the great happiness of the people. When I saw people who had so little to be happy about, living in an unshakable happiness, I was completely thrown. I was witnessing the miracle of simple man finding happiness in a rich inner world, not in the pursuit of some desired goal.*

---

*There is a fine story about Mother Teresa of Calcutta. A reporter was finally given an interview with the Roman Catholic nun who has made such an impact on India by caring for the poor and dying. Ushered into her simple room, the reporter burst forth, "Isn't it terrible, Sister. Ten thousand refugees are pouring into Calcutta every day from besieged Bangladesh, and there is no food or housing for them!" "No," replied Mother Teresa, "it is

Later I inquired into the origin of the word *happy* and found that it derives from the verb *to happen*. In other words, happiness is to be found simply from observing what happens. If you cannot be happy at the prospect of lunch, you are not likely to find happiness anywhere. What happens is happiness.

Simple man lives in this consciousness and finds happiness in a rich inner world, no matter what the outer circumstances may be. Men of enlightened consciousness know this noble fact and live in a philosophy and an attitude of happiness. For them, happiness bridges the inner world and objective fact, a connection that simple man is not capable of making.

Don Quixote, who will be the carrier of simple man in our inquiry, knows the colorful world of his inner life, his imagination, but he knows it at the expense of outer fact and reality. This way of life is rich and highly durable, but it requires a superior man to maintain it in the

---

wonderful. See, he just took food," pointing to the shriveled youngster in her arms who had just taken a spoonful of milk. A true saint, manifesting a form of enlightened consciousness, had seen a miracle and found hope and reason to live in that immediate fact. The reporter, quite certainly a man of complex consciousness, was lost in the terror and meaninglessness of the situation around him.

face of outer reality. Complex man, lost to the simple attitude of happiness and not yet understanding that God is what is, remains stranded in his worry, loneliness, and anxiety. A Hindu teacher once told me that the highest form of worship is simply to be happy. This happiness is known only to simple men and enlightened ones. Complex man, in between in consciousness, remains trapped by nostalgia for the past or anticipation of the future that mostly eludes his grasp.

Driven from the Garden

A whole generation of complex men have been thrilled and vicariously nourished by such books as *Zorba the Greek,* which portrays a wonderful earthy Greek who experienced the vitality of his life in a direct way, and by the novels of Hemingway, whose portrayals of bullfights and heroic living gave nourishment to pale, office-bound people.*

Because we have the unjustifiable opinion that complex consciousness is highly desirable,

---

*It was sad to see Hemingway himself fail his own vision and commit suicide when his own bravado was exhausted.

we very carefully educate our young out of their simplicity as early in life as possible. Parents are very proud if their youngsters can read and write or gain computer skills at a very early age. This often produces children who have been robbed of their childhood and been driven from their Garden of Eden much too early, and who therefore develop neuroses later in life.

Societies before the modern era and those still functioning in less-developed parts of the world believe that most people are to be left permanently in simple consciousness—in the Garden of Eden—unless they give solid proof of their ability to make their way through complex consciousness and on to higher consciousness. Thus, only a very few precocious individuals are allowed to acquire complex consciousness. Medieval Catholicism is often accused of trying to keep most of its people in a peasant state and allowing education only to those few destined to sainthood or priesthood. The Church censured Galileo not for stating a supposed falsehood, but for speaking the truth to those the Church considered unprepared to hear.

Complex consciousness is so highly prized in our society that no cost is thought too high to gain freedom, self-determination, and choice, the qualities of this level of consciousness. We are so zealous in championing complex consciousness that we will export its way of life to any other less-advanced country, free of charge!

Traditional Indian society is based on a caste system that allows only a few superior individuals to gain consciousness. These are the Brahmins, who are the priests, teachers, and mystics of Indian society. The next-lower caste consists of the rulers and warriors— people less concerned with consciousness. Castes lower than this are the domain of tradesmen and workmen. The system keeps the large majority of people in simple consciousness, with higher consciousness available only to those few individuals whose caste gives indication that they can survive the passage through complex consciousness. This system certainly has its flaws, of course. One of the most severe problems with the caste system is that it is hereditary and therefore does not always designate the individual to a level commensurate with his innate capacity. But overall it has avoided the mass neurosis prevalent in Western societies.

Our modern Western attitude toward consciousness has the great advantage of offering access to higher consciousness to virtually everyone. Anyone wishing to invest the necessary effort in consciousness is given the vantage point of complex consciousness from which to reach toward the highest level. But the difficulty of doing so leaves a large number of people stranded in complex consciousness, unable to proceed to higher consciousness or to return to the simplicity and peace of simple consciousness. Few people have the means or insight to become twentieth-century Thoreaus, even if they felt this was a viable solution. Dr. Carl Jung warns of attempting "to make a regressive restoration of the persona," to go back to a simpler consciousness when one has discovered the suffering of complex consciousness. Those who try this solution to the suffering of life merely put on a persona of simplicity, which is a further complication of an already overburdened life. Once you have left simple consciousness in favor of complex consciousness, you can never regain the simplicity of the peasant or "red-blooded" man. Returning to the Garden of Eden is not possible once you have been expelled from it, for, as Scripture informs us, there is an angel with a fiery sword standing there to refuse our return. Put more simply, you can't go home again.

In this book I want to explore the three levels of consciousness—which I have called two-dimensional man, three-dimensional man, and four-dimensional man—as they are portrayed in three works of literature. Cervantes, Shakespeare, and Goethe have given us works of art that portray these levels with great power. Cervantes wrote of Don Quixote, a man who was so enamored of the simple ways of two-dimensional man—medieval man—that he took on the finery of knighthood and chivalry and played out a half-comic but inspired imitation of what he had lost in his life. Shakespeare defined complex man with unerring accuracy in *Hamlet*. And Goethe gave us *Faust,* which picks up where Hamlet lost the battle and takes us on to that higher consciousness often called redemption.

In these three works we can trace the evolution of consciousness possible in this life.

1

Two-Dimensional Man:
Don Quixote

W e find a near-perfect representation of two-dimensional man—the simple peasant man—in the Spanish masterpiece *Don Quixote.* Written when Spain was leaving the medieval world in the early seventeenth century, the novel grew out of a Spanish legend. The qualities of youth and simplicity possessed by its characters have been all but lost to most modern-day three-dimensional men.

Don Quixote was written by Miguel de Cervantes, who was born in 1547, a man of no consequence if not for his novel. He lived a miserable life; in fact, it can be said of him, as of Marcel Proust, that he lived a failed life—and turned it into a masterpiece.

Cervantes had the genius of turning reverses into verses, a quality often seen in his hero. He fought in the battle of Lepanto in the eastern Mediterranean, lost an arm, was captured as a slave on the way home, and was ransomed and returned to Spain after five years of slavery under Moorish captors. He made a minimal living at various jobs, fathered an illegitimate child, later married a young girl of nineteen when he was fifty, then left her and lived in squalor in a single room for most of his old age.

In this unlikely setting he wrote *Don Quixote*. The novel is a definitive portrait of the medieval romantic troubadour who lived his two-dimensional life as if it were a mystical revelation straight from heaven. The book was an instant success, and pirated volumes quickly appeared from authors trying to share the income and fame. Cervantes wrote a second volume, which was of lesser genius, and died soon after, still in poverty and misery.

The story is about Don Alonso, an ordinary seventeenth-century Spanish man of not much education or position. At age fifty he has read so many books on chivalry and has grown so weary of his uneventful existence that he becomes enamored of the vivid, rich stuff of knighthood and chivalry. He takes the name Don Quixote, which is the term for that bit of medieval armor that covers the thighs and genitals. He is Sir Codpiece, a wonderful entry into the world of imagination. Do you remember the Fisher King in the Holy Grail legend who is wounded in the thighs?* Don Quixote is the unwounded one, since his armor covers that delicate part of his anatomy. Where the wounded Fisher King is suffering, groaning with agony, worrying, fretting, his wound incurable for most of his life, Don Quixote is free, optimistic, happy, and sure of himself. These are the chief characteristics of two-dimensional man, and we can only envy his assurance and certainty. Never having suffered the fall from the Garden of Eden, he retains the state of unconscious perfection.

The Archetypal Pair

Don Quixote takes a squire, Sancho Panza (the name means Mr. Paunch), and the two of them

---

*See Robert A. Johnson, *He: Understanding Masculine Psychology*, revised edition (New York: Harper & Row, 1989).

constitute an archetypal pair. Don Quixote is tall, noble of bearing, idealistic, and constantly searching for the *pan de trastrigo,* "the bread that is made from better than wheat" (a reference to the host of Holy Communion). Sancho Panza is short, fat, practical, immediate, and ruled largely by his appetite. In the Bible this pair turns up as Cain and Abel, Jacob and Essau, and David and Jonathan. Mutt and Jeff and Abbott and Costello are examples in our own time. It is ego and shadow, that pair of opposites in every psyche that differ in every aspect but are inseparable.

The poet W. H. Auden has written so brilliantly of Quixote and Sancho Panza that I would like to quote him at length:

> Without his comic lymphatic squire, the Knight of the Doleful Countenance would be incomplete. Sancho Panza's official motive for following Don Quixote is the promise of a governorship. But this is a purely imaginary idea to the former, and in the end he reveals his motives, which are (a) for the excitement, (b) for love of his master. Sancho Panza sees the world that requires changing as it is, but has no wish himself to change it. Yet it turns

out that he is the one who has to play
the part of the Knight Errant and res-
cue his distressed master from misfor-
tune. Don Quixote wishes to change
the world but has no idea what the
world is like. He fails to change anything except Sancho Panza's character.
So the two are eternally related. Don
Quixote needs Sancho Panza as the one
creature about whom he has no illusions but loves as he is; Sancho Panza
needs Don Quixote as the one constant
loyalty in his life which is independent
of feeling. Take away Don Quixote and
Sancho Panza is so nearly pure flesh,
immediacy of feeling, so nearly without
will that he becomes a hedonist pagan
who rejects everything but matter.
Take away Sancho Panza, on the other
hand, and Don Quixote is so nearly
pure spirit that he becomes a Manichee
who rejects matter and feeling and is
nothing but an egotistic will.*

Rocinante, an old hag of a horse (the name
means "she-whom-one-follows"), completes the
droll pair.

---

*Quoted in Lowry Nelson, Jr., ed., *Cervantes* (Englewood
Cliffs, NJ: Prentice-Hall, 1969), p. 80.

The Imaginative Journey

Don Quixote and Sancho Panza set forth to find Dulcinea, the sweetness of life, and to make the chivalrous journey that is the ideal of medieval man. Don Quixote admits under his breath that he is not sure Dulcinea even exists, but he vows to give his life for her. They never find Dulcinea, but she animates their journey from beginning to end. It is the fair lady who is the eternal quest of medieval man—whether she is real or not—as Don Quixote admits. She exists in the heart of the searcher, which is all that matters to two-dimensional man. He never tests this inner vision against outer reality; once one begins such testing, the two-dimensional quality is irretrievably lost.

Two-dimensional man lives constantly in the realm of fantasy and imagination, those infallible worlds that never fail one in an inner sense. They are the Garden of Eden, perfection, total reliability. They fail Don Quixote constantly in the outer world, and if you examine this story from the point of view of three-dimensional consciousness, it is a lesson in futility and childishness. Most modern people read *Don Quixote* in this manner, and treasure it as an exposé of medieval nonsense. If we can escape this prejudice even for a moment, we may find a world of inner reality in this masterpiece. Don Quixote is creating poetry, not reality. Heaven, love, idealism, hope, justice, chivalry, eternity—all are inner realities as palpable and real as any outer realities our world holds in such high esteem. Don Quixote's optimism ruins everything around him. But it finally proves to be correct. He loses every time he relies on his sword; it is his poetic imagination that is victorious. Don Quixote is "pure spirit disguised as fantasy," as Thomas Mann once wrote.* The true hero is a poet whether he likes it or not; for what is heroism if not poetry? This is the vision of two-dimensional man and is the stuff of nostalgia and fantasy for every three-dimensional man.

The Adventures

In the external world the adventures of Don Quixote and Sancho Panza appear to be episodes of failure. But Quixote is unbeatable because he seeks reality only on an inner level,

---

*Quoted in *Cervantes*, p. 53.

where it is always available. This is unacceptable to a three-dimensional man and so the two have no meeting ground. The dilemma can be bridged only by four-dimensional man, who is loyal to both inner and outer reality, but that is for later examination.

Let us follow the pair on two of their many adventures. The most famous one, of course, is the great battle with the windmills, the description of which deserves to be quoted in its entirety:

> At this point they caught sight of thirty or forty windmills which were standing on the plain there, and no sooner had Don Quixote laid eyes upon them than he turned to his squire and said, "Fortune is guiding our affairs better than we could have wished; for you see there before you, friend Sancho Panza, some thirty or more lawless giants with whom I mean to do battle. I shall deprive them of their lives, and with the spoils from this encounter we shall begin to enrich ourselves; for this is righteous warfare, and it is a great service to God to remove so accursed a breed from the face of the earth."
>
> "What giants?" said Sancho Panza.

"Those that you see there," replied
his master, "those with the long arms
some of which are as much as two
leagues in length."

"But look, your grace, those are not
giants but windmills, and what appear
to be arms are their wings which,
when whirled in the breeze, cause the
millstone to go."

"It is plain to be seen," said Don
Quixote, "that you have had little experience in this matter of adventures. If
you are afraid, go off to one side and
say your prayers while I am engaging
them in fierce, unequal combat."

Saying this, he gave spurs to his
steed Rocinante, without paying any
heed to Sancho's warning that these
were truly windmills and not giants
that he was riding forth to attack. Nor
even when he was close upon them did
he perceive what they really were, but
shouted at the top of his lungs, "Do not
seek to flee, cowards and vile creatures
that you are, for it is but a single
knight with whom you have to deal!"

At that moment a little wind came
up and the big wings began turning.

"Though you flourish as many
arms as did the giant Briareus," said

Don Quixote when he perceived them, "you still shall have to answer to me."

He thereupon commended himself with all his heart to his lady Dulcinea, beseeching her to succor him in this peril; and being well covered with his shield and with his lance at rest, he bore down upon them at a full gallop and fell upon the first mill that stood in his way, giving a thrust at the wing, which was whirling at such a speed that his lance was broken into bits and both horse and horseman went rolling over the plain, very much battered indeed. Sancho upon his donkey came hurrying to his master's assistance as fast as he could, but when he reached the spot, the knight was unable to move, so great was the shock with which he and Rocinante had hit the ground.

"God help us!" exclaimed Sancho, "did I not tell your grace to look well, that those were nothing but windmills, a fact which no one could fail to see unless he had other mills of the same sort in his head?"

"Be quiet, friend Sancho," said Don Quixote. "Such are the fortunes of war, which more than any other are subject to constant change. What is more,

when I come to think of it, I am sure
that this must be the work of the magi-
cian Freston, the one who robbed me of
my study and my books, and who has
thus changed the giants into windmills
in order to deprive me of the glory of
overcoming them, so great is the
enmity that he bears me; but in the
end his evil arts shall not prevail
against this trusty sword of mine."

"May God's will be done," was Sancho Panza's response. And with the aid
of his squire the knight was once more
mounted on Rocinante, who stood
there with one shoulder half out of
joint. And so, speaking of the adventure that had just befallen them, they
continued along the Puerto Lapice
highway; for there, Don Quixote said,
they could not fail to find many and
varied adventures, this being a much
traveled thoroughfare. The only thing
was, the knight was exceedingly down-
cast over the loss of his lance.

"God's will be done," said Sancho.
"I do believe everything that your grace
says; but straighten yourself up in the
saddle a little, for you seem to be slip-
ping down on one side, owing no
doubt, to the shaking-up that you
received in your fall."

Sancho then called his master's
attention to the fact that it was time
to eat.*

This episode of tilting with windmills has
been absorbed into nearly every Western language as a symbol of the folly of fighting with
phantoms or illusions. Outwardly, this is quite
true; but inwardly it is the imaginative heroic
battle of the child or simple two-dimensional
man. This battle has also been described in
terms of dragons, the monsters that every child
battles within his interior landscape. Of course,
there are no dragons, as everyone knows, but
people fall repeatedly under the spell of a
"dragon"—that is, a bad mood, usually origi-
nating in the unresolved psychological dy-
namics that men have with their mother
complexes beginning in childhood. It is this
heroic battle—with windmills for Don Quixote,
with dragons for another hero, with moods for
a modern—that is being fought out.** We may
laugh and smile at the childish imagery of Don
Quixote's battle, but on serious reflection it

---

*Miguel de Cervantes, *Don Quixote*, translated by Samuel
Putnam (New York: Viking, 1951), pp. 62–64.
**See *He* for further elaboration on such interior battles.

is no more bizarre than our own twentieth-century struggles. This is probably the reason we have so much empathy for Don Quixote: he is our selves served up to us in palpable form.

In another story from this imaginative medieval journey, Don Quixote enters a village where he sees a castle on the skyline. He complains that a page should blow a trumpet from the wall of the castle to announce the coming of one so high-born as himself. He imagines the horn call of a shepherd to be the royal trumpets announcing his arrival to the lord and ladies within. On the street he is met by several women of doubtful virtue, whom he hails as ladies of the court. A droll conversation ensues in which they try to ply their trade, but he treats them as the imaginary ladies of his fantasy. His courtesy is so strong and convincing that the women of the street are momentarily transformed into the courtly ladies of his expectation. Don Quixote and Sancho are taken to the local inn, where they find the fare to be a sumptuous banquet befitting their status.

Here again is the juxtaposition of inner reality and outer reality, with the inner vision triumphing over the outer. Three-dimensional thinking would find this story as ridiculous as the windmill episode; but viewed from the imaginative kingdom of the two-dimensional man, here are unshakable reality and romance and chivalry. The two-dimensional man lives in the triumph of inner reality over outer.

I once took part in a Don Quixote–like episode that taught me this principle. A young man brought his current girlfriend to meet me. The meeting limped along very badly with no one knowing quite what to say. I offered various bits of conversation but she would have none of them. After a time of very awkward silence she showed some interest in a lute that hangs on my wall. I put the lute in her hands and the awkwardness was resumed. Finally in desperation I tried a Don Quixote–like venture of observing that the young woman looked just like a Florentine painting of a woman holding a lute. This touched the magic of the two-dimensional world in her, and I learned the wonderful fact that if one will treat a woman like a lady she will respond by being one. The conversation flowed, and there was warm, interesting personal contact. My friend objected later, however, telling me that I had ruined their relationship. He complained that she was so busy being a Florentine lady holding a lute that she was interested in nothing else. Such is the power of inner truth.

The story of Don Quixote ends on a somber note. After numerous adventures of faith and heroism, the Don and Sancho Panza return home. Don Quixote lies dying. He now has a moment of lucid insight in which he sees that all his adventures have been unreal exercises of his imagination. He lays all this out before Sancho, who reverses his role and begins to argue that they should set forth again and begin a new search for Dulcinea. Surely this time, argues Sancho, they will find the sweet one and the knightly vision. Don Quixote dies. The last few hours of his life were lived as a three-dimensional man, part of the necessary movement toward higher consciousness. The true miracle of the story is the "sanchification" of Don Quixote and the "quixotification" of Sancho. The true journey of knighthood and chivalry has been to draw ego and shadow together, to diminish the split in personality indicated by the difference between the two, Don Quixote and Sancho Panza. Not much drama is made of this at the present level, but it will be crucial when we come to that intensification of the split personified by Faust and Mephistopheles.

We will see an example soon of another hero, Hamlet, who will spend the last moments of his life in the next higher stage of consciousness of which he is capable, that of four-dimensional man.

Backward and Forward: Cervantes and Shakespeare

Cervantes and Shakespeare occupied almost the same lifespan. In fact, they both died on the same day, April 23, 1616, by the Gregorian calendar.* *Don Quixote* was published in 1605, and the first edition of *Hamlet* was probably published in 1603 or 1604. It is as if the two men stood back to back, Cervantes looking backward and Shakespeare looking forward.

Cervantes pointed his genius backward and illuminated the medieval consciousness that

---

*Spain followed the Julian calendar in the seventeenth century, but England had adopted the Gregorian calendar, which was twelve days later. Consequently, the calendar dates of the men's deaths were twelve days apart. Obviously, the coincidence is not lost because of this.

was just ending in Europe. He constructed Don Quixote, the unwounded, un-self-conscious man of unshakable faith, the man for whom everything works in poetic terms, outside the vicissitudes of reality. Cervantes spoke of the childhood of Western man, man who had not yet suffered the shock of being expelled from the Garden of Eden. No better description of two-dimensional man can be found.

Shakespeare, in *Hamlet*, looked forward and made a statement about the modern man who was to come. It is to that play that we now turn for insight into three-dimensional man.

2

Three-Dimensional Man:
Hamlet

In examining *Hamlet* we come to a very dark chapter in this book. Don Quixote, with his roots deep in instinct and faith, is the man of courage who redeems anything that befalls him. In Hamlet we find the man of tragedy, he who makes chaos and failure of everything he touches. Hamlet is torn man, tragic man, suffering man, "sicklied o'er with the pale cast of thought." He is the opposite of Don Quixote in nearly every respect. Hamlet is the most profound example in all of literature of the divided man. Only Dostoevsky's characters come close to equaling him in their dividedness.

Cervantes brilliantly portrayed medieval man as he left the stage of European civilization. Shakespeare foretold the modern, worrying, anxious man who was to take the center of that stage and is still the model for our character. Most people today are Hamlets, caught in that dry place between Don Quixote, who was never at a loss for something bright and cheerful in life, and Faust, that man of higher consciousness, a state yet to come for most men.

To understand Hamlet is to gain invaluable insight into the emptiness and loneliness of modern existential life. Hamlet is three-dimensional man: he has no roots in the instinctive world and his head is not yet in the heavens, where he can gain the nourishment of enlightenment. He is the forerunner of a new man whose characteristics will be the healing of the paradox of masculine and feminine, doing and being. Lao-tse, the Chinese sage, commented on this: "He who understands the masculine and keeps to the feminine shall become the whole world's channel. Eternal virtue shall not depart from him and he shall return to the state of an infant."* Hamlet's fail-

---

*This is Lao-tse's description of the perfect state or the Garden of Eden. Quoted in Harold Goddard, *The Meaning of Shakespeare* (Chicago: University of Chicago Press, 1960). p. 333.

ure is that while he touches this divine state, he makes only division and tragedy of it, not paradox and synthesis. (We must wait for Faust to evolve in this way.) If Hamlet has a failing, it is his inability to withstand the pressure of the herd mentality that surrounds him.

He cannot make up his mind whether to follow the dictates of custom and its barbaric solutions or to listen to the enlightenment of his own soul and conscience. He does neither, and finally he loses the value of both. But Hamlet, in his losing, is the forerunner of *Othello* and *King Lear,* and, most of all, of *Faust.*

The Exile

The play begins with Hamlet exiled from his rightful place as king of the land. His father has just died and Hamlet's uncle, the usurper, has taken the throne. Worse, the usurper has married Hamlet's mother within a month of her widowhood.

Hamlet's friends bear the news to him that a ghost haunts the ramparts of the castle at midnight. Hamlet attends the ghost. He hears the voice of his father exclaiming that he has been murdered most foully and that Hamlet must take revenge to claim his rightful place as king. Hamlet's undoing begins with endless uncertainties. He debates within himself whether he should kill the usurper, which would have been his right as a medieval king, or listen to the more noble part of his heart and not add more blood to an already bloody drama. Finally he does neither. As Emily Dickinson once put it, "He wavered for us all." It is this vacillation that is his undoing and that characterizes a three-dimensional man.

In seeing Hamlet fail to make up his mind—paralyzed between two paths—we see the impossibility of living as a three-dimensional man. "A thought which, quartered, hath but one part wisdom and ever three parts coward" is Hamlet's diagnosis of his malady. The terrible, unlivable lot of the three-dimensional man is to see the "fourness" of life—its wholeness—severed into two unequal parts, three and one. He has sight of the four, the wholeness, but has only three of its parts functioning. There is no peace in such a man. He knows too much to be simple, but not enough to be whole. It waits for Faust, who uses precisely the same language of three and one for healing, to take this theme to its completion and heal the wound of self-consciousness.

I am reminded of the arrow that pierced the Fisher King's thigh in the story of the quest for the Holy Grail. It can neither be drawn back out nor pushed through. So it stays in, festers, and exposes its bearer to unending suffering. Hamlet cannot shake himself loose from his paralysis; his need to act and his abhorrence of violence are in conflict.

Out of this agony Hamlet utters the most famous soliloquy in all of literature:

> To be, or not to be, that is the question:
> Whether 'tis nobler in the mind to suffer
> The slings and arrows of outrageous
>   fortune,
> Or to take arms against a sea of troubles
> And by opposing, end them. To die, to
>   sleep—
> No more—and by a sleep to say we end
> The heartache, and the thousand
>   natural shocks
> That flesh is heir to; 'tis a
>   consummation
> Devoutly to be wished. To die, to
>   sleep—
> To sleep—perchance to dream—ay,
>   there's the rub,
> For in that sleep of death what dreams
>   may come

When we have shuffled off this mortal
   coil,
Must give us pause.*

This is the cry of despair and imprisonment that haunts every three-dimensional man. Hamlet, the very epitome of the uncertain man, cannot make up his mind whether to live or die! He cannot live; he dares not die. He tortures everyone around him, especially the women close to him, and makes life unbearable for himself. A lesser man might have burst his way out of the dilemma by killing the usurper uncle; a greater man might have withdrawn from the struggle and found a solution through fate and faith. This is not to imply that killing the uncle would be wrong; Hamlet's indecision is the irredeemable element. A Chinese proverb has it, "If you are going to stand, well stand; if you are going to sit, well sit. But don't wobble." Hamlet wobbles, wavers, and edges toward his destruction.

His own confession is:

O that this too too sullied flesh would
   melt,

---

*William Shakespeare, *Hamlet,* in *The Riverside Shakespeare* (Boston: Houghton Mifflin, 1974). All quotations are from this edition.

Thaw, and resolve itself into a dew!
Or that the Everlasting had not fix'd
His canon 'gainst self-slaughter! O God,
    God,
How weary, stale, flat, and unprofitable
Seem to me all the uses of this world!
Fie on't, ah, fie! 'tis an unweeded
    garden
That grows to seed.

As Tolstoy wrote, "He was suffering the anguish men suffer when they persist in undertaking a task impossible for them—not from its inherent difficulties, but from its incompatibility with their own nature."

Polonius, Hamlet's intended father-in-law, gives him advice that could avert all the coming tragedy; but Hamlet cannot hear: "This above all, to thine own self be true, and it must follow as the night the day; thou canst not then be false to any man."

Hamlet's indecision finally drives Ophelia, his beloved and the daughter of Polonius (who Hamlet later kills), to such a state of suffering that she utters a desperate cry:

My lord, as I was sewing in my closet,
Lord Hamlet, with his doublet all
    unbrac'd,

No hat upon his head, his stockings
    fouled,
Ungart'red, and down-gyved to his
    ankle,
Pale as his shirt, his knees knocking
    each other,
And with a look so piteous in purport
As if he had been loosed out of hell
To speak of horrors—he comes before
    me.

Hamlet, when challenged about what he is doing, replies, "Words, words, words." Three-dimensional men are often caught in words and are hesitant to act. At one point Hamlet cries, "Now to my word." Another hero, Faust, will take up the problem of the word later and realize he must also act.

R. H. Blyth, the literary critic, comments: "This 'words, words, words' has a deeply tragic meaning in the play. It is, in fact, the secret of Hamlet's character, the cause of the tragedy. Hamlet is the Zen-less man, whose energy, like a mouse in a wheel, goes round and round inside him and issues, not in action, but in talking."*

---

*R. H. Blyth, *Zen in English Literature and Oriental Classics* (New York: E. P. Dutton, 1942), p. 140.

Hamlet is so alienated from the feminine beauty of his inner life that he utters this famous blasphemy to Ophelia: "Get thee to a nunnery, why wouldst thou be a breeder of sinners? I am myself indifferent honest, but yet I could accuse me of such things that it were better my mother had not borne me."

He then adds insult to the injury:

> If thou dost marry, I'll give thee this
> plague for thy dowry: be thou as chaste
> as ice, as pure as snow, thou shalt not
> escape calumny. Get thee to a nunnery,
> farewell. Or if thou wilt needs marry,
> marry a fool, for wise men know well
> enough what monsters you make of
> them. To a nunnery go, and quickly
> too. Farewell.

It is characteristic of complex man, caught between functioning by instinct and acting by enlightenment, that he often destroys everything feminine within his grasp. We watch Hamlet destroy Ophelia, for what woman or what feminine element could withstand such abuse? We see Hamlet destroy the queen, his mother, with equal devastation. All feminine elements wither in the face of three-dimensional consciousness.

The Poisoned Rapier

Hamlet finally decides on a most clever device for making his intentions known to the usurper king. A group of players arrives at the castle, and Hamlet instructs them to produce a play in which a noble king is murdered by poison, following which the murderer takes the throne and marries the murdered king's wife. The usurper king, upon seeing the play and comprehending its message, plans Hamlet's death.

Hamlet goes to the usurper king's chamber with full intent to kill him and set right the "something [that] is rotten in the state of Denmark," but he finds him at prayer.

> Now might I do it pat, now 'a is a-
>   praying;
> And now I'll do't—and so 'a goes to
>   heaven,
> And so am I revenged. That would be
>   scann'd:
> A villain kills my father, and for that
> I, his sole son, do this same villain
>   send
> To heaven.

Hamlet backs away, again uncertain. The king, finishing his prayers, says: "My words fly up, my thoughts remain below: Words without thoughts never to heaven go."

Ophelia's brother, Laertes, surveys the growing tragedy as he observes his sister's suffering. Ophelia, finally borne down by this artless indecision and tension, drowns herself in a stream.

The king now instructs Laertes, who is Hamlet's friend, Ophelia's brother, and the son of the murdered Polonius, to engage in a friendly fencing duel with Hamlet but to put poison on the tip of his rapier so that he, by an accidental thrust, might kill Hamlet. A stoup of poisoned wine is nearby in case the poisoned rapier does not do its deed.

The duel is fought and Laertes wounds Hamlet, but then an exchange of rapiers takes place and the poisoned rapier, now in Hamlet's hand, wounds Laertes. Laertes, in the face of death, confesses what has been done. Now Hamlet takes action: he rises out of his indecision and strikes the king with the poisoned rapier. But it is too late. The queen, unseen by those around her, drinks the poisoned wine and dies. In a moment Hamlet, the king, Laertes, and the queen are dead of the indecision that feared any action and by so fearing brought down the worst possible outcome on all. Killing and death are the result of Hamlet's efforts to avoid a decision that would have cost him only a fraction of the final cost.

A few moments before his death, Hamlet comes to an awareness of a consciousness beyond his neurotic split and indecision. Just as Don Quixote saw the three-dimensional consciousness at the last moment of his life, so Hamlet sees that which is greater than himself at the last moment of his life. He says:

> Our deep plots do pall. And that should
> learn us
> There's a divinity that shapes our ends,
> Rough-hew them how we will.

The play ends with the tender lines of Horatio, a noble and solid person:

> Now cracks a noble heart. Good night,
> sweet prince,
> And flights of angels sing thee to thy
> rest.

Hamlet is the man of nobility and partial consciousness who sees a vision of the meaning of life. But he is not strong enough—or complete enough—to bring that vision into focus. He is wise enough to see but not strong enough to accomplish. He is caught between vision and practicality and fails in both regards. In this he is the prototype of so many modern men who see a noble world in their imaginations but don't have the means to accomplish it.

Hamlet fails, but he fails so that Faust might begin where he left off. We turn now to the story of Faust to find a solution to the problem that overwhelmed Hamlet.

3

Four-Dimensional Man:
Faust (Part I)

The simple man (Don Quixote) enjoys his secure relationship to life, which is natural, happy, and safe. This precedes a stage higher on the evolutionary scale represented by Hamlet, the worried, anxious, driven, and unhappy man who can conduct his life only tragically. Fortunately, there is a guide to lead us out of the morass of the three-dimensional man's self-consciousness to the enlightenment of the four-dimensional man. This guide comes from Johann Wolfgang von Goethe (1749–1832), the German Shakespeare, who wrote his masterwork, *Faust,* as a thinly disguised autobiography.* The story of Faust is an old one, but it describes the dilemma of modern Western man so exactly that it becomes a lifeline for us.

The Shadow

Hamlet's basic error was his failure to incorporate his shadow or dark side into his working life. If Hamlet had been able to acknowledge as an ally the "red blood" of his instinctive nature, he would have shaken loose from his paralysis. Instead, he stayed poised between his two natures, ego and shadow, and died a tragic death.

Faust picks up where Hamlet lost the battle and provides a solution for us to this most modern dilemma. He finds his way out of this paralysis by interacting with his shadow, Mephistopheles, until each has been redeemed. The story of Faust is one of the great statements of optimism, hope, and redemption in Western literature.

---

*Johann Wofgang von Goethe, *Faust,* translated by B. Q. Morgan (New York: Macmillan, 1954). All quotations are from this edition.

Faust is the story of a highly complex, intelligent man who must come to terms with his dark side. The play begins with a prologue in heaven that would be unbearable were it not taken very closely from the Book of Job. God and the devil are having a conversation; they are apparently on familiar terms with each other, and they converse easily. They are talking about creation. God asks how humanity is faring. The devil replies, "Oh, very badly, the worse for your having given them reason." God inquires specifically about his servant Faust. The devil reports that Faust is doing very badly, is utterly miserable and suffering terribly. God and the devil then make a wager. The devil asks God to permit him to divert Faust from "the path that is true and fit." God replies, "Faust will not succumb to your temptations. He will stay true," and the devil replies, "I wager that he won't."

This wager in heaven is the prototype of the wager made between Faust and Mephistopheles a little later in the play. It is sobering to find that this split between the ego (Faust) and the shadow (Mephistopheles) is an archetypal reality and is not just local in origin with individual man.

The Inflated Man

The story begins with Faust, a middle-aged college professor, just becoming wise enough to know that he knows nothing. He has reached the pinnacle of success—the highest position possible for him—but finds himself alone, unrelated, his life meaningless. Goethe once commented that if a man raises his head to the stars, then the clouds play with his feet. When one's "reality function"—the "feet-on-the-ground" ability—is threatened, an encounter with the dark side, Mephistopheles, is the corrective.

Faust has known intuitively that he would come to this point of hopelessness and, in anticipation of this terrible moment, has kept a vial of poison in the back of his desk drawer. One day when his feelings of loneliness and meaninglessness reach an unbearable point he retrieves the poison.

This is a terrible moment in the life of an intelligent man. He now sees that his level of consciousness, his perspective on life, will not support him. He has explored discipline and self-consciousness only to find them a dead end. This exploration is absolutely essential in one's evolution, and the man who has not trodden that road is not eligible for the moment of despair that is also the moment of redemption and enlightenment. This is the midlife crisis, the mute suffering of existential man, the dark night of the soul. This is the experience of the intelligent man, the heroic man, the one who has reached the goal of modern consciousness. This is what happens when you reach the top of the ladder only to find that it was set up against the wrong wall. It is the very best man who suffers this Hamlet crisis. Lesser men take refuge in guilt at their inadequacy, or blame their environment, or find yet another set of windmills to vanquish—anything but face the terror of seeing that three-dimensional consciousness is not bearable, no matter how finely developed it is.

It is a compliment of the highest order when a man finds that he cannot go farther and that his life is an irredeemable tragedy. His ego consciousness is stalemated, and this stalemate is the only medicine that will drive him out of the Hamlet tragedy and inspire him into a new consciousness.

A fault of this magnitude cannot be repaired, but can be healed only by finding a whole new level of consciousness from which to function.

Hamlet, the ego-centered man, fails; Faust, who learns a center of gravity greater than himself, redeems that failure. If one were a genius the process would be inspirational, but for most of us it is experienced as the torture of the end of the rope. This divine/hellish point is the critical moment that can make or break the rest of a man's life. Hamlet fails at this moment; Faust, with the goading of his shadow, Mephistopheles, finds a correct way.

The Perennial Music

Just as Faust is about to drink the poison and end the unendurable suffering of his isolation, he sees and hears a vision of Easter music. A heavenly choir appears and so inspires him that he forgets the poison and rises to a new understanding and consciousness. The Easter music Faust hears is available to any person, but it generally takes a great crisis before the ego of an ordinary Westerner is humble enough to hear that perennial music.

Faust sets the poison aside and goes to mingle with the festival crowd outside his study. He dances with a peasant girl, accepts a stein of beer, and draws close to the ordinary world, which only moments before had seemed so alien to him. For a man who has been locked up in his "Hamlet isolation" for half a lifetime, the experience of human warmth and closeness is a reprieve from hell.

If you can wait just a little longer when you reach the terrible moment of the dark night of the soul, the Easter music *will* burst forth. For Faust, the first appearance of the vision is brief—the length of a dance with a peasant girl and the draft of one stein of beer—but it is promise enough to save him.

Kafka once said, in a moment of anguish, that the Second Coming of Christ would happen the day after the end of the world. This is also true of that moment of utter collapse in a man of three-dimensional consciousness just before the first redemptive vision of four-dimensional consciousness breaks through. Kafka could not wait that one day in between the two levels, so he remained in despair. It is not uncommon for men to get stuck in this no-man's land. It is a holy place but an exceedingly dangerous one. Suicide is common, and it is easy to slip into despair or the solace of madness. It is a high compliment that one should experience this existential anguish, but it is also a terrible danger. The fact that our culture has lost most of its guidelines for people at this point of their evolution makes it all the more difficult. For these guidelines, we turn to *Faust*. It is certainly not the only set of guidelines for this journey, but it is a product of the Western mind and is couched in terms that we can understand. It is a fresh statement of an ancient art, which gives it special relevance today.

The Black Poodle

Faust is refreshed, has found new energy to support him, but then he does exactly the wrong thing with this energy. Faust's assistant, Wagner, Mr. Dry-as-Dust, calls him to go back to his dry, isolated study and resume his work, and Faust responds, returning to the very life that had dried him up and led him to despair. But as Faust and Wagner reenter their study, a stray black poodle that has attached itself to Faust worms its way in through the door between their feet. Faust's shadow has been made visible and given physical form and will not be shaken off. What a strange result from a heavenly vision!

We are conditioned to think that a great vision will bring angelic experience, creativity, delight; it does, but its most salient effect is to constellate the shadow! The conscious hope is for angelic things, peace, love, creativity; but it is the shadow that brings the energy to live as a human being. No one can be anything but a partial being, ravaged by doubt and loneliness, unless he has close contact with his shadow. The shadow consists of those aspects of your character that belong to you but that have not been given any conscious place in your life. Faust has gamboled too long in the empyrean heights of thought and abstraction and theory. It is the black poodle, a symbol of his shadow, that will make life possible for him. Assimilating one's shadow is the art of catching up on those facets of life that have not been lived out adequately.* Wholeness implies that we must find those parts of ourself that are missing in life.

It is wonderful moment when the black poodle enters Faust's study. Faust has a shadow

---

*A person of very different character from Faust—say, someone who had not developed his intellectual or studious side—would find his shadow in the very realm that Faust has to leave. A very earthy person, for instance, might have to give attention to his intellectual side.

now through which God can touch him and redeem him! The black poodle makes redemption possible. This truth cuts so strongly through our sentimentalized thoughts about goodness and redemption that many people flatly refuse to believe it and automatically stunt their spiritual development for the rest of their lives.

There are now three in the study, a far more powerful combination than just two. The poodle will bring energy and paradox, both of which are necessary for redemption. In fact, there is so much energy in the room that as the poodle moves about the study, flames leap up from its footprints on the stone floor. This is not unlike the manifestations of Shiva that are so often accompanied by flames in Hindu mythology. Shiva is the Indian God of destruction, certainly a carrier of paradox for a Western mind. It is only when creation (Brahma) and destruction (Shiva) are both present that wholeness is possible.

The Missing Energy

Faust decides to do some work—a regression to his old way of life—but even this is enlivened now. Dissatisfied with the translation of the beginning line of the Gospel According to John, he sets to work on a new translation. "In the beginning was the Word" is precisely the one-sided attitude that has brought such inertia to Faust, and it is this perspective that he now challenges. He strikes upon a new attitude for the beginning of his gospel, "In the beginning was the Act," and a whole new consciousness of life opens up to him. It is difficult to comprehend at first glance what a change in attitude, what an expansion of consciousness the alteration of this one word can make. The lifelong scholar who has lived by words now embraces the world of action and finds a whole new dimension of life.*

At the moment when Faust changes the text from "Word" to "Act" the poodle is so excited and energized that it races around the room, leaving footprints of flame. Then it disappears behind the old tile stove that is part of

---

*Lest we take this as formula it must be noted that if this were the story of a man who had lived all of his life by the rule of action, he would have to make the sublime discovery of the world of words. Encountering the shadow means rediscovering the unlived faculties of one's life, not following any prescribed formula for change.

every German study and emerges as Mephistopheles, his lordship, the devil!

When your shadow finally becomes incarnated, there is often a huge influx of energy. This is the return of the vitality that was missing in Hamlet, the man of three-dimensional consciousness. It has also been missing in Faust because of his one-sided life as the man of "word" rather than "act." But the problem is far from solved. His lordship, Mephistopheles, announces himself as "part of the part which was once the whole." This hints at the work that is to be the task for the rest of the story. Humanity's original wholeness must be restored and reinstated. This cannot be accomplished by going back to an earlier stage of consciousness. The attempt to "go back" or romanticize the "good ol' days" is a common political theme in American culture. It usually marks the desire to avoid difficult times ahead, and of course it is always a lie. Nostalgia means business profit but psychological disaster. You must go forward from the Garden of Eden, through the painful time of transformation, to the heavenly Jerusalem, which is a symbol for the wholeness of man restored.

The Pact

Mephistopheles greets Faust, after which they enter into the famous contract, which is to restore youth and vitality to Faust for twenty-four years. This contract is the center of the Faust story, and it is worth examining carefully because it reveals the nature of Goethe's genius.

Christopher Marlowe's play *The Tragedy of Dr. Faustus*, written in the late sixteenth century, gave a traditional presentation of the pact. Simply, Faust was to pay for twenty-four years of restored youth by yielding his soul to the devil. In the last scene of Marlowe's version, Faust is led away into the flames of hell by a triumphant Mephisto. A terrifying prospect— to lose your soul for a few years of youthful vitality.

Goethe's version of the story, however, adds a provision to the pact. Faust is told that if at no time along the way he says "Linger, thou art fair," he will be free at the end of the twenty-four years. In other words, if Faust can experience the unlived life of his youth but not become attached to any part of it, he is free!

Unlike Marlowe, Goethe teaches that the unlived life (and who does not have a huge store of
unlived life following him like a reptilian tail?)
can be caught up, restored, recovered, and
experienced without doing basic damage to
one's inner life. Faust indeed causes a great
deal of damage in his Mephistophelean journey,
but he can remain safe spiritually if he refrains
from attachment to any of his experiences.
This is a spiritual truth so profound that it
takes years of observation before its full impact
can be comprehended.

The Opposites

So off they go, Faust and Mephistopheles, a pair
as opposite as black and white. The tension
between them alerts us to the most important
lesson in *Faust:* that *all* of one must be redeemed! It is not a matter of the triumph of
one part of oneself over another. At the beginning of *Faust* the two partners are as unlike
each other as possible. At the end they have
tempered each other until they are nearly
indistinguishable. The point of the Faustian
transformation is that opposites temper and

restore each other, rather than one overcoming the other. At the beginning of the relationship Faust is weak, shy, frightened, and inept; Mephistopheles is ruthless and bold, without morality or ethics. At the end of the play, Faust has become strong and Mephistopheles has learned to love. Such is the true transformation of a pair of opposites: tempering, not triumph.

A long series of adventures occupies the middle of the play. Briefly, the pair go to a tavern where Faust, for the first time in his life, experiences what it is like to be an irresponsible youth. He doesn't think much of the experience; it is not fascinating, as he had imagined it might be. Mephistopheles replies that he promised Faust youth and experience, not happiness. Faust begins to wonder about his bargain.

Then they go to a witches' kitchen where Mephistopheles brews up a concoction that will make Faust fall in love with the next woman he meets. Faust soon meets Gretchen, a girl so pure that Mephistopheles mutters, "What can I do with a girl on her way home from confession with nothing to confess?" Mephistopheles schemes to change this by wooing Martha, Gretchen's friend, who quickly succumbs to

Mephistopheles's advances. Finally Gretchen, who is vulnerable to Martha's example, consents to being courted by Faust.

Faust succeeds in seducing Gretchen. Soon she is pregnant and in her childlike way utterly dependent on Faust. Gretchen's brother, Valentine, a soldier just home from the wars, sees the situation clearly and challenges Faust to a duel. He is killed by a sword thrust that Mephistopheles has taught Faust.

Mephistopheles then takes Faust to the witches' sabbath, where every form of sensual nonsense rages out of control. Faust is miserable with this and complains to Mephistopheles that he is having no pleasure or happiness. Mephistopheles once again reminds Faust that he promised youth and vitality, not happiness.

Faust returns to find that Gretchen, blinded by her misery and shame, has killed her newborn child and committed suicide. Faust is utterly miserable and rages at Mephistopheles, who replies, "Well, was it you or I who got Gretchen pregnant?" Faust realizes that his newfound freedom and youthfulness has created little but destruction. Part I of *Faust* ends in profound but conscious suffering.

The Longing

There is a terrible lesson to be learned from Part I. It is a chronicle of the hungering of a middle-aged man for the youth he missed. And what modern person does not have a large measure of life unlived in him as he approaches the midpoint of his life? To take the hungering of his unlived life literally is to fall into the tragedy of Part I of *Faust*. There are not enough Adidas shoes, Hawaiian shirts, or exercise machines in the world to fill the middle-aged man's longing for his lost youth. Civilization has cost us a huge portion of unlived life in payment for the high specialization it represents. Any civilized person pays a price for the culture and civilization he has wrested from the raw material of his character. To attempt to live out these unlived sections of ourselves literally is to fall into Faust's error and end Part I of our lives in depression and misery. Few misconceptions of modern man cost him so heavily as this tendency toward literalness. If Goethe understood this in the early nineteenth century, it is a hundred times more urgent for us to understand it today.

The American ideal of perpetual youthfulness dies very hard in us. We are so materialistic and so enamored of the power of will that we refuse to relinquish what is irretrievably out of our reach. The lesson of Part I of *Faust* is a sobering and inescapable fact: there is no literal solution to unlived life. The water that has passed under the bridge has indeed passed us by forever in any external sense. If *Faust* were to stop at this point it would be a gospel of such despair that it would have much the same effect upon us as Goethe's earlier work *The Sorrows of Young Werther*. Many a copy of this book has been found beside a suicide.

A lesson of great value can be had from *Faust*, Part I. The problems of meaninglessness and loneliness, the results of our unlived lives, can be made conscious. This is a painful task, but it sets the stage for what we need to learn in Part II, the best guide in Western literature for resolving the Faustian dilemma.

The Imaginative Realm

As George Bernard Shaw observed, "There is no alternative in life to torture except fine art." We can find an alternate interior environment for experiencing and integrating our lost youth in the realms of symbol, ceremony, art, and imagination. These languages exist apart from time and space.

Hearing them can bring the Easter music again, allowing Faust to be permanently absorbed into it later in his life. Thus far Faust has only seen one brief vision of this superpersonal realm, just enough to keep him from despair, the separateness that had fallen upon him. A man caught in the early stages of three-dimensional consciousness finds a little nourishment in the remnants of his two-dimensional consciousness (sport, play, adolescent behavior, closeness to nature, adventure, hero worship); so also a man at the close of his three-dimensional consciousness can get a small trickle of nourishment in the anticipation of his four-dimensional consciousness. Faust's vision of the Easter music was such an experience. It is the dead center that is so dangerous when one is shut off from both the two- and the four-dimensional worlds—that terrible day Kafka spoke of that sits between the end of the world and the Second Coming of Christ.

This dilemma is voiced in Nicodemus's question to Christ: "Must a man enter into his mother's womb a second time?" Christ replies, "No, except a man be born of the water and the spirit he cannot see the Kingdom of Heaven" (John 3:4–5). This is to say that man cannot be redeemed from his unfulfilled life by any literal rebirth but he can be redeemed by the water and the spirit, the world of imagination and symbol.

The Horrible Tangle

Imagination and symbol make up a realm of experience in our interior lives where the ego is important but not dominant. Inner work requires that the ego consent to a subordinate, but still important, role. With inner work you take part in a process in which every element of life, including the dark elements, has a place of dignity and worth. Without the ego, chaos would erupt. With the ego in control, you are blocked by the egocentricity that marred Faust in Part I. Faust ran the show in Part I and made a horrible tangle of the process, as the ego always does when it is in control. When faced with this dilemma, men are tempted to adopt a new kind of egocentricity in which they use their powers of dominating the world for "spiritual" purposes. This is no less egocentric than any previous use of the ego, and it constitutes a particularly vicious trap on the path. Further progress is not possible unless you realign your ego's place in your life. Jung described this moment of realignment as the relocation of the center of gravity of the personality. This process is so painful, since it consists of dethroning the ego, that it is rarely done.

The process requires that you give honor and dignity to every dimension of your life. The Christian version of the incarnation of God in Jesus Christ provides a valid example of this. Though the fact is frequently ignored in our modern world, Christianity gives equal validity to the human and the divine dimensions of Christ. Any variance in this balance is fatal to spiritual growth and is also the basic definition of heresy in the Church. Most of us live in heresy, even if the concept is mostly discredited now, by giving dominance in our lives to one principle over all others. It is the unity of life, not the triumph of one faculty over another, that is the goal of imagination, fantasy, and ceremony.

4

Four-Dimensional Man: *Faust (Part II)*

Part I of *Faust* leaves us with no solution to the Faustian dilemma, but it does force the dilemma to consciousness. Faust is a suffering but conscious man at the end of Part I. Though he has no idea what to do about his dilemma, he has become far more aware of his condition than he was at the beginning of the play.

Goethe spent most of his adult life writing *Faust*. He published Part I in 1808, when he was fifty-nine years old. He then worked steadily at the continuation of the play but did not allow Part II to be published until after his death in 1832.

Part II is an expression of the symbolic working of man's soul. It is written in the language of imagination, a kind of alchemical treatise, a fairy tale, a myth. It is only on this level that Faust can find a way out of his imprisonment in three-dimensional consciousness. The efforts of planning, reasoning, discipline, and heroic ventures would only further the emotional confusion of a man who has attained the degree of consciousness Faust has at the end of Part I. Again, it is only in the realm of symbol and ceremony that the solution can be found.

The Symbolic Experience

Part II opens with a scene in the emperor's court. Gold making is in progress; there is a great deal of heat, fire, and energy, but it is not certain that any gold has been produced. A boy charioteer mounts a horse and gallops off furiously, never to be heard from again. This is the first gift—pure undifferentiated energy—of the *puer,* the inner child of every man.

When a man consents to begin the interior journey, the symbolic quest, he may expect certain characteristic experiences. For a sojourner in this nearly trackless land to have even a general knowledge of these coming events can be encouraging.

A great deal of energy is produced when one touches a symbol or a symbolic experience. Emotions flare up, fear and exhilaration alternate, and inflations are extremely common. If you come to the emperor's court, a symbolic place deep in the unconscious, you must have enough emotional stability to withstand the intense heat and the strangeness of the journey. A guide or teacher is of inestimable aid.

The figure of the *puer aeternis,* the eternal youth, is central in this journey. Since the journey is largely outside the laws of the three-dimensional world of time and space, it is not surprising that the archetype of the *puer aeternis* is activated. The *puer* energy in a man is that eternal inner child whose mentality is geared to the fantasy and whose eye is on heaven rather than on any practical endeavor. Some men don't integrate this energy maturely and as a result they go through life as dreamers. But those very inner-child qualities are Faust's salvation. He has worn out his three-dimensional world and needs a vision of heaven to draw his shattered world back into coherence.

The First Puer—The Charioteer

Four *puer* figures appear in Part II of *Faust* and none of them are very practical. However, it is around these four figures that the necessary evolution takes place. The first is the boy charioteer who gallops off at full speed. Any man embarking on this symbolic quest must understand that he will be swept into one enthusiasm after another. Such enthusiasms soon wane and are forgotten. These senseless enthusiasms can be discounted but for the fact that they provide the energy for the mystic vision. This vision is the salvation of a three-dimensional man.

After this energetic but inconclusive episode, Faust makes the extraordinary demand to see Helen of Troy. Finally, he has the intelligence and perspective to ask for a vision of beauty and femininity, which Helen symbolizes. Mephistopheles outlines the way in which this request can be fulfilled, and it is at the very heart of Faust's transformation from a time-and-space-bound consciousness to the next level, which we often describe as holy, redeemed, enlightened, eternal, or visionary. Mephistopheles instructs Faust to go to the place of the Mothers in the eternal depths, insert his key into the tripod, and by this means summon Helen of Troy.

Few sentences in the history of consciousness say so much in so few words. Go to the depths, the place of the Mothers, and place the key in the tripod. This is the most concise instruction for making your way out of the three-dimensional world when you are ready to move on to mature spirituality.

Going to the depths indicates that the experience is profoundly inward and solitary. Mephistopheles may not accompany Faust on this journey; he must go alone. The journey requires extreme introversion, an inward turning, forty days and nights in the desert.

Going to the place of the Mothers is an act of regression, a psychologically incestuous act. If done indiscriminately this would be fatal for consciousness, but when done intelligently it can be the opportunity for salvation. The place of the Mothers is where consciousness and cultural and spiritual power originate. Returning to your origins and generating or regenerating yourself is the act of creating consciousness. An old alchemical saying proclaims: "I find myself, I mate with myself, I generate myself, I gestate myself, I give birth to myself, I am myself."

Our evolution thus far has been based on the rather tenuous observation of two-, three-, and four-dimensional levels of consciousness available to men. Now we have a direct mythic statement that the third level may be turned into the fourth by adding the key to the tripod. This is critical for the evolution of Faust, as indicated by the following lines from the play:

Faust:
> All right! We'll try it out! In what you call
> Sheer nothingness I hope to find the All.

Mephistopheles:
> I'll praise you now before you start your trip:
> You know the Devil to his fingertip.
> Here, take this key.

Faust:
> That little thing!

Mephistopheles:
> Grasp hold! It's not the trifle that it seems.

Faust:
> It grows beneath my hand! It glows! It gleams.

Mephistopheles:
> You see what great advantage it can bring?
> The key will scent the right place and skip
> others;
> Follow it down, it takes you to the Mothers. . . .
> Sink, then! I could as well say:
> Rise! It makes no difference.

From forms developed flee
Into realms which are from forms set free!
Rejoice in things long vanished from our eyes,
Whose files, like cloud processions, wend their
way;
Brandish the key and hold them all at bay.

Faust:
Now as I clasp it tight, new strength be mine!
My heart expands; now for the great design.

Mephistopheles:
A glowing tripod last of all will show
That you have reached the deepest depths
below,
And by its gleam the Mothers you will see,
Some seated there, or as the case may be.
And make your way straight to that tripod's
light
And touch it with the key.

The use of tripod and key is a literary device
to indicate the addition of the one to three. This
results in the four, the consciousness that is the
true goal of humanity. By working most of a
lifetime at the task of civilization, an educated,
intelligent man has erected a "tripod" of life.
This is something similar to the Christian con-
struction of the Holy Trinity. Both are symbols
of a consciously constructed way of life that is
cultured and civilized but inevitably leaves out

the fourth element. Christianity raised a fine trinitarian structure but had to reckon with Satan or the devil as the neglected element. Civilization has raised high culture but it now must reckon with its shadow or dark side as the neglected element. It is the addition of the neglected element that brings an individual or a culture to wholeness.

The Evolution of Three to Four

Jung was fascinated by the evolution of consciousness represented by the number three moving to four. He spent his later years on this subject and his last several books are occupied with this phenomenon. He saw that the number three represented a consciousness that was time-dominated, devoted to acting, doing, processing, accomplishing. We live in an age that holds a trinitarian view of theology. The doctrine of the Holy Trinity is basic to the Christianity of our time, and the Holy Trinity is an exact model of our modern consciousness. The number four, though, denotes being, eternity, peace, and contemplation. Dr. Jung never tired of pointing out that we live in an age where the collective unconscious is devoted to the evolution from three to four. Virtually every modern person is drawn into this evolution and dreams of these symbols. Often the dreams directly involve three turning into four, though it is extremely rare that people have any conscious awareness of what this process involves or means.

If our civilization is to negotiate the perilous years immediately ahead, it will be by virtue of this evolution. Dr. Jung was often asked if we would make it. He always replied, "If enough people will make the necessary evolution within themselves," the evolution of consciousness, which is so often pictured as the evolution from three to four.*

For most people, the transition from three-dimensional to four-dimensional consciousness is exceedingly painful. Medieval Christianity called it the dark night of the soul; Dante called it the journey through hell and purgatory; it was forty days and forty nights in

---

*It is fascinating to me that three great figures of the twentieth century occupying almost exactly the same lifespan—Carl Jung, the scientist; Teilhard de Chardin, a Catholic theologian; and Sri Aurobindo, a Hindu mystic—each talked of a new consciousness and new world order, though each spoke in the language of his own discipline.

83

the desert for Jesus; it was a journey in the belly of a fish for many a hero.

For a modern man it is midlife crisis or, worse, a nervous breakdown; or still worse, physical suicide. The process can be summed up in one sentence: it is the relocating of the center of the personality from the ego to a center greater than one's self. This superpersonal center has been variously called the Self, the Christ nature, the Buddha nature, superconsciousness, cosmic consciousness, satori, and samadhi. This relocation appears to be death when viewed from the perspective of the ego. Zen masters observe that satori (their term for a nonpersonal center of consciousness) can be viewed by the ego as nothing but total disaster. And death it is! The ego loses its supremacy and goes through a short time of violent suffering.

When someone threatens suicide at this time, I caution him that he must be very careful to do it *without* harming his body. The relocation of the center of the personality is a form of suicide, and it's best done voluntarily by the ego. Meizumi Roshi, a Zen master in Los Angeles, once said, "Why don't you die now and enjoy the rest of your life?"

There is a story about this process in Shakespeare's *King Lear.* Gloucester, who has been cruelly blinded and shorn of all his worldly possessions, power, and family, is wandering in misery on the dark, wet moorlands of England. His loyal son, disguised as a peasant boy, has come to protect him. Gloucester begs the peasant boy to take him to the cliffs of Dover so that he might hurl himself off and end his misery. His son takes him to the center of a field and convinces the suffering old man that he is on the edge of the cliff, and Gloucester hurls himself over the "edge" only to land in the middle of the field in which he was standing. But so great was his suffering that he thinks he has gone over the cliff, and so now he stands up enlightened and relieved of his suffering. He recognizes his son and utters some of the most sublime lines in literature. Gloucester did his "suicide" correctly.

The Ordinary Life

Faust has won a vision of Helen of Troy by taking his perilous journey into the maternal depths. It is as if when he touches the great maternal feminine he unlocks the greatest feminine beauty, Helen of Troy. But Faust immediately blunders in a highly instructive way, if we heed it.

Faust tries to embrace Helen of Troy, to have a personal relationship with her, but there is a huge explosion, Helen vanishes, and Faust is left lying unconscious on the ground. Faust is burned and nearly destroyed by attempting to have the wrong kind of relationship to the archetypal world. It is not terribly difficult to open up the unconscious; almost anyone can do it. But it is exceedingly difficult to enter into a relationship with the superpersonal forces that this unleashes. When you have earned your enlightenment at the cost of the deep inner journey, your first reaction is often to personalize this experience, to own it somehow. As Jung observed, if you have an assimilating match with a tiger, you know who will assimilate whom. Faust makes a serious mistake, as do most people who travel this far on their inner road. Archetypes and archetypal energy are bigger than we are; we cannot try to embrace that energy without causing a psychological explosion.

Mephistopheles is helpful at this moment and gently carries Faust back to his dusty study for a bit of ordinariness. The word *ordinariness* is derived from *ordered,* and ordinariness is the very best medicine for inflation or egocentricity. To embrace that which is ordinary can restore us to human dimensions and can purge the inflation. Wagner is in the study, and together he and Mephistopheles restore Faust. Wagner, who has not occupied an attractive place thus far in the story, shows his usefulness now. That which is dry, pedestrian, and bookish can have a healing effect at critical moments. An iconoclast needs to learn that a little reason and discipline are not hindrances on his way to heaven.

The Second Puer—The Homunculus

Wagner, Mr. Dry-as-Dust, has been busy with his alchemy and has magically produced a homunculus—a man the size of a thumb. This man-made creature, the second appearance of the *puer aeternis,* has the wonderful power of serving as a guide back to ancient Greece, to which Faust is delighted to have access. Like

India today, ancient Greece had close contact with the dark elements of life and with the gods and goddesses that represented these forces, but it had no concept of evil comparable to our own. It is nearly impossible for a Western man to imagine a society that has no concept of evil. It is also a remarkable experience to be in such an environment. India has a trinity of gods, with a fourth quite outside that trinity, a structure similar to our own Trinity and devil. Brahma, Vishnu, and Shiva occupy the noble trinitarian positions, while Krishna is left to carry the earthy side of things. In this scheme Krishna corresponds to our Christian devil. But what a vast difference! Lord Krishna is a happy adolescent with sixteen thousand wives. He spends his time sporting with the Gopis, who are the milk maidens of heaven.

There is no place for evil in this cosmology, just as there was no place for it in ancient Greece. Mephistopheles finally finds a place for himself there when he discovers a concept of ugliness, the closest possibility to his own nature. He comes along as a hideous old hag with one tooth and one eye.

The homunculus, being a magical creation of man, explodes in a blinding flash when it encounters the Greek ideal of beauty. None of our human ideas of beauty and nobility hold up in the face of archetypal beauty.

The Third Puer—Euphorion

Faust awakens to find himself in his beloved ancient Greece and has another chance to relate to Helen of Troy, the ultimate expression of feminine beauty. This time, with more caution and in a setting more worthy of the magnitude of the meeting, Faust is allowed to make a less personal and brief marriage with Helen. They immediately produce a full-grown youth, Euphorion, who is the patron of art. His energy can produce inspiration and artistic expression. This is the third appearance of the eternal boy, the *puer aeternis.* Euphorion immediately flies up to the heavens to get the tools of the poet for Faust. But, like Icarus, he flies too close to the sun, burns his wings, and falls impotent into the sea. The *puer* has again tried to help, but his limitations and his vulnerability to inflation and egocentricity are now clear.

It is the universal experience of one on the path to grasp at the tools of genius when he encounters these sublime realms. Pain often compels us to think, "Nothing personal has worked well in my life, so I will write. That will be a realm where I can express myself." This is basically correct. But in fact the old self, the three-dimensional man, tries to do this in an egocentric way and therefore his efforts are doomed. This is not to say that you should not write or paint, but you must understand that your first attempts will be so ego-contaminated that they will catch fire and fall into the sea like Euphorion.

Faust is learning, however, and a sublime event now occurs. Faust embraces Helen of Troy but she slips out of his grasp. Mephistopheles whispers to Faust, "Hold onto her garment, which will carry you above the commonplace." Helen of Troy vanishes, the great archetypal vision fades away, but she has left enough of herself to activate the artistic, visionary faculty in Faust. And this lesser way of possessing Helen is not too much for mortals to bear. When you know at what level and in what manner you can relate to the impersonal archetypal world, you are truly safe. Then creation can begin.

This may seem only a tiny sliver of your first vision, but that is quite enough to bring into the everyday world. Many an artist has failed his calling because he refused a limited, less-than-perfect expression of his original vision. A man cannot handle the great artistic tools of the boy-god Euphorion, and he may not be able to embrace the superhuman vision of pure beauty, Helen of Troy, but a man can touch Helen's garment, which is sufficient to bring a small part of his artistic vision into creation. To do more would burn us up in gigantic inflation.

Reclaiming the Land from the Sea

The drama is nearing its end, and Faust and Mephistopheles are drawing closer; each has tempered the other, each has healed the other. Mephistopheles feels his demonic power over Faust diminishing and makes a rather feeble effort to regain control of Faust. He asks if there is anything that Faust would like. "Nothing," replies Faust. The insatiable man, "whom infinity would scarcely satisfy" at the beginning of the play, has come close to contentment and peace. Much healing has taken place. "Would you not like to have the moon?" asks Mephistopheles. "No," Faust replies; but he asks for a piece of coastline so that he might reclaim land from the sea. Water, particularly the ocean, is a universal symbol of the unconscious, and Faust is asking for eternal connection with the depths represented by the sea.

The true work of man in the latter part of his life is the cultural process of bringing up some of the contents of the unconscious and integrating them into consciousness.* This is the process symbolized by reclaiming land from the sea. Mephistopheles arranges this quite easily for Faust and we soon find him dredging canals, building dikes, taking land from the sea and adding it to the land mass. He is happy and content with this project and is deeply absorbed in it. He finally has attained some measure of peace.

Then a horrible event takes place that is hard to interpret. An old couple named Baucis and Philemon have lived all of their lives in a little cottage on Faust's newly acquired land. Faust feels they obstruct the view. He complains to Mephistopheles, who frightens the old couple to death and burns their cottage to the

---

*See my book *Inner Work: Using Dreams and Active Imagination for Personal Growth* (San Francisco: Harper & Row, 1986) for further elaboration on this theme.

ground. Faust is horrified but realizes that he himself is responsible for the brutal act. Mephistopheles replies, "The couple did not suffer much." As Faust grows more aware of what his alliance with Mephistopheles is costing him, he learns that he has power over Mephistopheles and that he is capable of misusing that power.

Faust is growing old, nearing the end of his life. While preoccupied with reclaiming land from the sea, he fails to see four gray sisters approach. Want, Debt, Need, and Care appear at his side. These dark forces are the power of necessity. Faust's wealth makes him immune to three of them, but not to Dame Care, as no man is. When Faust refuses to take this dark force seriously, she blinds him. Faust then returns to his work of reclaiming land from the sea. This leads me to believe that the blinding was more an inner exchange of sight for insight, a transformation required of every man as he grows old.

Soon Faust's excavation becomes the digging of his own grave, since his lack of sight has cost him all awareness of what he is actually digging. You can recognize here one of the dangers of old age: you dig or hack away at a project more out of inertia and habit than out of any sense of purpose.*

A moment before Faust's death he steps back from his labors, sees a utopian vision of a noble band of free people inhabiting his newly claimed land and—horrible!—utters the fatal words, "Linger, though art so fair!" Mephistopheles rushes in triumphantly and claims Faust's soul, according to the terms of their contract twenty-four years before.

Faust has lost and Mephistopheles has won! Is the terrible truth that life is to be lived, only to be lost by a very human slip at the end? Is absolute perfection required of us at the gates of heaven? It seems to be Faust's fate to be denied entrance to heaven, but then two wonderful and seemingly miraculous events occur

---

*A Hindu story tells this in a striking way. A young man prayed fervently to the gods for his enlightenment. One of the gods incarnated and instructed the young man in the disciplines necessary to attain his goal. The young man practiced diligently for ten years and finally earned his enlightenment. The god came again to confer the great gift upon the young man. When he tapped him on his shoulder to transfer the precious gift, the young man snarled at him, "Go away! Can't you see I am busy?" A time comes when even your most noble activity must stop if you want to receive a more precious gift. This is not a matter of retirement but of cultivating a faculty of discernment.

that save both our protagonists. Gretchen, whom Faust had treated so badly, has persevered in her love for him. Because of that she appears at the head of a choir of angels to plead for Faust's release from Mephistopheles. They beg at the gates of heaven, pointing out that it was a vision of heaven, not anything that Mephistopheles had produced for him, that caused Faust to utter the fatal words. This seems a slender argument, based as it is on a technicality, but Faust is saved and, led by Gretchen, enters into heaven in a flood of light. Finally, at the gates of heaven, it is grace, not justice, that prevails. The masculine stuff of law and order and justice are superseded by grace and love.

The Fourth Puer—The Boy Angel

We have seen no redemption of one in a pair of opposites is possible without the same redemption for the other. This law functions here and validates the dual process of redemption. Both Faust and Mephistopheles have to be redeemed if either is to find wholeness. As I have also said, the only redemption for either of a pair of opposites is the tempering of one by the other. We watch the process of the Faustianization of Mephistopheles and the Mephistophelization of Faust.

Mephistopheles, muttering, angry at his loss, catches sight of a boy angel in the heavenly band, falls in love with him, and forgets to press his partially legitimate charges against Faust. To understand the multitude of forms in which love may touch you is to gain some sense of its great mystery. Mephistopheles has been touched by that form of love that is specific to his need and his transformation.

Faust is redeemed by the love of Gretchen; Mephistopheles is redeemed by his first experience of love. Ego and shadow each finds its own level of redemption and its own appropriate salvation.

The boy angel, symbolizing love, is the fourth manifestation of the archetype of the *puer aeternis,* and sums up the power of that figure. To touch the *puer* is to touch eternity, to touch love, and to be delivered from the time-space world that India labels as *maya,* or illusion.

The play ends with these sublime lines:

All that is perishable
is but an image;

Here the short-reaching
becomes result.
The indescribable—
here it is done;
The Eternal Feminine
draws us on.

This is more than a hint that wholeness is not attained by means of masculine law or contract. It is a gift from the eternal feminine aspect of God. Faust is saved by the very bungling of his attempts at love, by his perilous journey to the place of the Mothers, and by the fidelity of Gretchen.

No less miraculously, his lordship, Mephistopheles, that dark part of our human capacity that we call the devil, is saved by the first stirrings of love within his dark bosom.

Conclusion

D on Quixote, Hamlet, and Faust have taken us on a sublime journey from simple man to enlightened man. It is the journey of every man of consciousness and should not be dismissed as fairy tale or myth. Every man is somewhere on this journey, and it is of immeasurable help to know where you are on the scale of evolution. To mistake one's position might be to take medicine that is inappropriate and possibly fatal.

Almost all of us in Western society are Hamlets. Compulsory education, our social structure, the dictates of our lifestyle have obliterated the two-dimensional man from American life. He lives in our passion for American Indian stories, in the novels of ethnic New York, and in our devotion to the cowboy. Except as pathology, he is rarely seen on our streets in adult form. A friend once described adolescents as the last primitives among us, for the two-dimensional man does live there for a brief time. America has a love-hate relationship with adolescence, obliterating it by urging youth to become adults as rapidly as possible and simultaneously bearing an unquenchable nostalgia for it.

How does a man survive if he is caught in the Hamlet dilemma? The more intelligent he is, the more profound will be his suffering. Two avenues of solace are available. He may keep some small point of contact with a simple, warm, uncomplicated world by maintaining a bit of primitive behavior in his life. At best this can be jogging; camping; engaging in locker-room banter; having an array of adolescent equipment, including that which is most dear to every man's heart, his car (every car should be named Rocinante); gardening; or reclaiming some dimension of life ordinarily relegated to the store or shop. Its dark form—the second avenue of solace—can be vandalism, gang behavior, and other types of juvenile delinquency, including drug use. It is a bitter indictment of some of our attitudes that the only "juice" left for many of our youth is in destructive behavior. But inevitably a time comes in adulthood when these small sources of simple energy dry up and you face the dark night of the soul when there is no joy in jogging and your garden is defeated by the insects. This is the terrible moment when the full Hamlet distress comes welling up in you. We have invented new terms for this: midlife crisis, identity crisis, the Big Four-Zero, the seven-year itch. It is a dark time when the small connection with boyish exuberance dries up.

St. John of the Cross said that this dark time lasts seven weeks or seven months or seven years or twenty-one years—depending on when you wake up to the next level of consciousness. Some information and a profound integrity can save a man from the very long dry times; but no one escapes at least a touch of the dry desert.

When the dark night begins to lift, one morning there is an unaccountable touch of joy in the air. It is the tiniest trickle of energy, light, and hope, but enough to keep you alive. This is the first contact with the four-dimensional consciousness, and one can begin to live from that source of energy. Something of the subtle inner world becomes your center of gravity: poetry, music, a new perceptiveness when you are jogging, a blossoming of philosophic inquiry, a new religious understanding—something of this world captures you. Less worthy channels for this new energy are fanaticism, dictatorial religious beliefs, and ego inflations of all kinds. If the new energy flows into such channels, you are quickly sent back to the Hamlet condition for further boiling in the oil of transformation.

Enlightenment is never total or permanent in this lifetime. Mythology has to construct personalities who are perfect, but they always live somewhere else or at some other time. Presently the evidence of four-dimensional consciousness is not some form of perfection but rather the ability to tap in to that psychological space when needed.

I have been touched deeply to learn that the ability to perceive the color blue is a recent acquisition for the human race—it probably developed fewer than two thousand years ago. The word *blue* does not appear in the Old Testament or in Homer (who speaks of the "wine-dark sea"), or any of the classical writings. This ability emerged slowly, and blue is still the most often missed hue in color blindness.

Similarly, the musical sense of hearing harmonic structure—as opposed to melodic line—is probably still more recent; harmonic music appears only in the fifteenth or sixteenth century. Is it consistent to say that a new faculty—four-dimensional consciousness, as we lamely describe it—is only now appearing for ordinary men and women in our human evolution? If this is so, it would follow that the new faculty is extremely rare, fragile when it does appear, and very easily lost. But it has made its appearance and is the most important issue in any intelligent life. Dr. Jung spent his old age writing about and contemplating this new evolution of man, the progression from incompleteness to wholeness, from three to four. It is time for all of us to do the same.